RECONNAISSANCE:
New & Selected Poems & Poetic Journals
2005-2015

Other Books by Mark Pawlak

Natural Histories (Červená Barva)
Go to the Pine: Quoddy Journals 2005–2010 (Plein Air Editions/
      Bootstrap Press)
Jefferson's New Image Salon: Mashups and Matchups (Cervena Barva)
Official Versions (Hanging Loose)
Special Handling: Newspaper Poems New and Selected (Hanging Loose)
All the News (Hanging Loose)
The Buffalo Sequence (Copper Canyon)
Poems: Richard Edelman & Mark Pawlak (West End)

Anthologies by Mark Pawlak

*When We Were Countries: Poems and Stories by Outstanding High School
      Writers,* Co-editor (Hanging Loose)
Present/Tense: Poets in the World (Hanging Loose)
Shooting the Rat: Poems and Stories by Outstanding High School Writers,
      Co-editor (Hanging Loose)
Bullseye: Poems and Stories by Outstanding High School Writers, Co-editor
      (Hanging Loose)
Smart Like Me: High School-Age Writing from the Sixties to Now, Co-editor
      (Hanging Loose)
Something to Say: A Boston Worker Writers Anthology, Co-editor (West End)

RECONNAISSANCE:
New & Selected Poems & Poetic Journals
2005-2015

Mark Pawlak

Hanging Loose Press
Brooklyn, New York

Published by Hanging Loose Press, 231 Wyckoff Street, Brooklyn, New York 11217-2208. All rights reserved. No part of this book may be reproduced without the publisher's written permission, except for brief quotations in reviews.

www.hangingloosepress.com

Printed in the United States of America
10 9 8 7 6 5 4 3 2 1

Hanging Loose Press thanks the Literature Program of the New York State Council on the Arts for a grant in support of the publication of this book.

Cover design: Marie Carter

Cover art by Jean Holabird. "North Haven Ferry," ink and pencil, 4.5" x 6". Notebook entry 7/03/15.

ISBN 978-1-934909-83-6

Library of Congress cataloging-in-publication available on request.

. . . one becomes,
sometimes, a pair of eyes walking.
. . . walking and looking,
through the world,
in it.
—Denise Levertov, *Sands of the Well*

The question is not what you look at, but what you see.
—Henry David Thoreau, Journal, 5:VIII:1851

To Mary and Gianni

Table of Contents

IV. Go to the Pine

I. In Transit

I put these down in my ledger,
Charles, walking and watching,
which is the way we serve.
  —Harvey Shapiro, "For Charles Reznikoff"

Meanwhile

Next bench over from mine
in this park just off Harvard Square,
a professor in tweeds,
newspaper open on his lap,
sips coffee from a paper cup.
Beneath his seat
an oblong cardboard box
shelters someone still asleep.
From where I sit: just two boot soles visible.

Meanwhile, across the street,
in the recessed doorway of a shop soon to open,
a young man lies curled on sheets of newspaper,
cherubic face in the crook of his elbow,
around him three tall plastic cups ranged like votive offerings:
dregs of stale beer in one,
black coffee in another,
cigarette stubs in the third.

Meanwhile, just blocks away,
students in residence halls now start their day
with only cold cereal for breakfast
or so one news story reports,
and at faculty meetings professors have had to forgo
the cookies traditionally served with their tea—
belt tightening has reached the Ivy League.

Meanwhile, the street corner is already bustling.
There an early bird sitting on his overstuffed gym bag
has staked his claim. In tee-shirt and shorts,
bandanna wrapping his head,
with magic marker and cardboard

spread flat on his lap, he's working up
a sign to advertise services:
"DESERT STORM VETERAN.
WILL WORK FOR CASH."

Among the Colleagues

Before descending into the subway's maw,
before facing the mess on my desk:

Shop grates drawn, sleepers stretched out on benches,
in doorways, just beginning to stir,
but already someone with a broom has gathered
fallen buds into neat piles on the square's red bricks:
heaps of fairy goblets on long green stems
left over from yesterday's celebration—
Morris dancers in knickers,
jangling ankle bells, clacking sticks.

Already this early, at his coffee shop station,
the self-appointed doorman:
straggly hair, beard, gray, flecked with white;
paper cup in one hand—
patrons drop in their coins, no words exchanged;
his vest and trench coat bulging with rolled newspapers,
slips of paper crumpled in shirt pocket—is he
bum, bard, or bodhisattva?

Yesterday: I saw red-eyed Sappho stumble along the sidewalk
oblivious to the crush—office workers headed home—
her gaze downcast, mumbling verses as she passed shops
with pansies in window boxes and recessed doorways:
from their shadows satyrs and sirens, her familiars,
leaned forward, greeted her. This morning
leather-skinned Li Po staggers past, scattering pigeons,
ending a night filled no doubt with wine and song.
Strands of hair peeking from under knit cap,
he lurches from this lamppost to the next,
embraces one as a long lost friend,

spits curses—"Motherfucker"—at another
as at a sworn enemy, "Motherfucker."
Early "patrons" at tables of the not-yet-open outdoor café, my confrères:
ruddy-faced men in hand-me-down work boots,
coats half-buttoned, sweatshirts showing beneath:
White-bearded Walt Whitman shares a cigarette
with someone who could be his twin.
Nearby, Basho, tonsured, in need of a shave,
scans yesterday's headlines,
at his feet two plastic bags stuffed with only he knows what.
And, just back from the west, Po Chü-i
sits under a shade tree in new leaf,
his one crutch propped against the trunk,
scribbling poems on scraps of paper,
which he neatly folds, stuffs into his breast pocket.

Finally, here is portly Marx!
parked beside cardboard boxes of books in a shopping cart, his
      movable library,
signature beard splayed on chest,
eyes fixed on a book propped open on his belly,
deep in conversation with himself—something just audible
about "oil prices . . . simpler times . . . bosses . . . "
one moment serious, holding up both sides of the argument,
the next chuckling to himself, amused.

Before descending into the subway's maw,
before facing the mess on my desk,
such, these May mornings, such is the company I keep.

With Apologies to Rilke

Du mußt dein Leben ändern—
"Archaischer Torso Apollos,"
Rainer Marie Rilke

1. 5 A.M. Dark:

Ruckus of house sparrows
nesting in bedroom air conditioner,
tinkle of porch wind chimes,

kitchen fridge hum, toilet flush,
water coursing through pipes,
gurgle & burp of coffee maker,

heels clacking against
hardwood floor downstairs,
distant church bell's gong . . .

distract, but only momentarily,
from the mice gnawing
in my mind's attic—

Ich muß mein Leben ändern!

2. T Station:

"Boss?"
one *Metro* hawker
is saying to another

as I hurry past
to catch my train.
"Boss?

I ain't got no
boss. I got
supervisors.

I got supervisors.
I ain't got
no boss."

3. Red Line Inbound:

Eyes wander to banner ads
pasted above windows across aisle.

One, in bold lettering, inquires,
"Do you worry a lot?"
        Yes, I admit
        I do.

"Feel nervous most of the time?"
        Unh-hunh.

"Feel anxious in social or performance situations?"
        That's me.

"Have distress, flashbacks, or nightmares from trauma?"
    Not from "trauma."

"Are you ANXIOUS?"
    Bingo!

"Call 866-44-W-O-R-R-Y."

Ich muß mein Leben ändern!

4/ Square

For Ralph Fasanella *in memoriam*

1.

Slant early morning light
on empty city square,
empty but for pigeons,
inspecting paving stones
for flawed workmanship

under the watchful
half-open eye
of the woman
who sleeps in an alcove,
rat's nest of hair for her pillow.

2.

Outside the coffee shop, a man is changing out of bedclothes, as if
in the privacy of his own dressing room, his wardrobe spread out on
two benches and a chair. He pulls tee-shirt on over union suit, then
hooded sweatshirt over that, followed by a sweater, then another, then
a checkered wool shirt on top that he meticulously buttons all the way
up, oblivious all the while to pedestrians hurrying toward the T stop,
shopkeepers turning keys in locks, storefront grates noisily going up
behind him.

3.

Man hunched over
outdoor café table,

muy scruffy,
but not scrofulous,

wearing a straw hat
frayed at the brim,

sits nibbling
breakfast pastry

while perusing his newspaper
that's folded neatly beside him:

CHESS LESSONS $2

Nervous sparrows at his feet
peer upward,

awaiting crumbs
to drop from his beard—

the Master and his Disciples.

4.

7:10 AM

Three ruddy-faced, boon companions, two men and a woman, sit together on a bench, outside the coffee shop, beside improvised cardboard bedcovers, conversing while rubbing sleep from their eyes. (One asks me for the time as if he had an appointment to keep.) They exchange greetings with the cop nearby on hard-hat duty where new paving is being laid; then offer comments on the passersby hurrying to work or subway, men and women in suits, in pressed shirts and slacks or blouses and skirts, most with cell phones raised to ears. Roving gangs of sparrows scavenging for muffin crumbs hop excitedly on grass patches bordering the path that cuts diagonally through. (One, at my feet, cocks its chestnut head, begging a handout.) Their shrill cheeping is drowned by the rumble and thrum of delivery trucks shifting gears, accelerating, one of which has three-foot high green lettering stenciled on its side:

TROPICANA
PURE PREMIUM
Not from concentrate

Faith, Hope, Charity

Street corner morning, sidewalk littered:
plastic soda bottles, candy wrappers, aluminum cans—
flotsam after yesterday's snowmelt.
When the light's red, a man
(paper cup in hand, winter coat unbuttoned)
steps off the curb
into the sunlit lane between stopped cars.
Cradled in the crook of his arm
an improvised sign:
SEEKING HUMAN KINDNESS,
ALL MAJOR CREDIT CARDS ACCEPTED.

Inside the coffee shop,
a line of patrons stretching from counter to threshold
waiting for pastries and morning java. Just outside,
three anxious sparrows twittering beneath the bench
where a young man sleeps, stretched out,
duffel bag for a pillow,
face turned away from us passersby.
Beside him some Samaritan has left
a lunch sandwich,
neatly wrapped in clear plastic, homemade.

As I descend into the subway station,
the ever-cheerful *Metro* hawker greets me: "Have a nice day."
At the Dunkin' Donuts kiosk
a dark-skinned man—West Indian?;
curly gray hair under
the knit cap he wears in all seasons,
cargo bags at his feet,
hunches over a Bible
open on a pedestal table, his "lectern."

Some days he scribbles in a notebook—sermons?—
other times, lips moving, eyes turned inward,
he recites passages to himself. Today, he lifts his head,
casts his gaze over the multitude,
hand extended, and, citing chapter and verse,
silently preaches to his congregation
entering, exiting through the turnstiles—
to all of us sinners and to no one in particular.

Inbound/Outbound

Forbidding Charles Street Jail's
ancient granite edifice,

undergoing renovation,
glimpsed from inbound Red Line train:

large, white banner
draped from scaffolding

announces in bold, black letters,
"Future Site of the Liberty Hotel."

★

Young Black woman,
hair pulled back tight with a clasp,

body-hugging sweater, skin-tight jeans,
high leather boots with stiletto heels,

walks briskly down the subway platform
past the *Metro* hawker.

"You look," his words trail after her,
"like an Egyptian queen."

She pays him no mind. "You ARE
an Egyptian queen."

★

Unshaven, middle-aged man
standing on wobbly legs

before the subway escalator, transfixed,
uncertain whether to descend,

not willing or unable to retreat—
the pavement beneath his feet

regurgitating stairs
one after another after another.

★

Haze-softened early morning light
of this soon to be searing-hot day;

runners along the riverbank,
scullers on the Charles in singles and eights;

grassy park seen from the inbound bus,
freshly mown in alternating shades of green,

where, on benches, two scruffy young men
are packing up bedrolls and sundries,

before shambling to the Square
to panhandle for their breakfast.

★

Overheard

You know why it's called KFC don't you?
> You mean instead of Kentucky Fried Chicken?

Right. They can't use the word "chicken."
> Why not?

On account of how they breed them in their factories.
> How's that?

All breasts and drumsticks; no heads or feet.
> Headless chickens?

Yep.
> I don't think so.

Yes, really!
> Nah.

Yes!
> Nah.

★

Gaunt, white-bearded mannequin
in ratty car coat, worn jeans, sneakers,

gray strands of hair showing under the brim of his porkpie hat,
stands mute and motionless, staring blankly ahead

as morning commuters scurry past
down the ramp, leading from bus drop to subway.

The white cardboard sign held up at his chest,
hand lettered in bold capitals,

reads:
H-E-L-P.

★

Suit, pressed white shirt, bow tie, and brogues,
standing legs akimbo on the rush hour train:

opens his *Wall Street Journal* with snap
as if to shake out chaff,

then folds back the page along the crease,
smooths with one hand the top sheet,

adjusts half-moon reading glasses
resting on the bridge of his nose,

gets down to the business
of business.

★

Take Me Home

Female street musician
standing on subway platform at rush hour,
guitar case open at her feet
into which commuters awaiting trains,
myself included,
have dropped coins, a few bills.

Chinese or Korean,
she strums and sings
in heavily accented English,
over and over, just the chorus
of John Denver's "Country Roads:"
Take me home
To the place
I belong . . .

Her tongue wrestling to enunciate
the "l"s, the "r"s
West Virginia,
Mountain mamma,
Take me home
Country roads.

★

Man riding the outbound train,
shod in paint-splattered work boots,

blurts out, "Look at this!"
to fellow passengers, standing and seated;

to no one in particular; "Look at this!"
pointing to his newspaper.

"It says right here, 'four American coots
spotted in Braintree yesterday.'"

Hands open, palms turned up,
he lifts his shoulders

in a gesture of puzzlement:
"Four American coots . . . what's the big deal?

I see American coots
every single day."

★

Movie poster ad

Cropped photo of young woman's face,
full lips parted, teeth bared,

whose rheumy eyes stare
through cross-hatched wire fence or cage—

Hollywood's image of dangerous sex;
her feral glare fixed

on the business-suited, young man —
white shirt, striped tie—standing before her,

gripping the horizontal bar on this
crowded, lurching, rush hour train.
The movie's title: *Captive*.

★

Police Action

Train idled in tunnel due to "police action" somewhere up the line. Man across aisle, unfazed by the announcement, keeps eyes fixed on library book open on his lap. I take him for a teacher—junior high, maybe high school: casual jacket, slacks, dress shirt and necktie under crew neck sweater; but is he? Could it be a disguise? Surveillance photo posted above his head of T riders in a car just like this one; its caption asks: "Can you identify the police in this picture? How about on this train? Just because they're not dressed like Police, doesn't mean they aren't."

Earlier in the station, cops standing before turnstiles conducted random searches, while loudspeakers broadcast the daily mantra: "If you see something, say something," meaning shopping bags left "unattended" on or under seats; pocket books, briefcases, backpacks . . . meaning keep watch for suspicious behavior; meaning trust no one.

Train moving again pulls into the next station. Young woman enters; finds seat; opens newspaper. I scan the headlines from across the aisle. One reads: "The officer in uniform is real; but his badge may be an impostor." Meaning what?

Train stands idled in station with doors wide open. Bomb-sniffing canine enters, straining at leash. Its cop/handler follows: black shirt, black vest, black pants tucked into high-laced black leather boots, handgun in holster on his hip; packing handcuffs, Mace, "persuader." They walk the car's length, exit to platform at other end, raising new questions, answering none. Doors slide closed; train moves out. Crackle of loudspeaker again: "If you see something, say something."

★

Overheard: Two Teens on Bus

What are we learning?

I'll tell you:
about electrons.

They're so small
you can't see 'em.

So, you tell me,
why do I need to know?

★

Vet

Memorial Day cemetery flags,
threadbare fabric

wrapped tightly around thin dowels
capped with gilt finials,

bundled and lashed tightly with cord
to an overstuffed backpack

that leans against this alley wall
behind the Post Office,

where in adjacent brick niche
a lumpy cocoon,

goose down and olive-drab nylon,
lies zippered up—

with what chrysalis inside,
dreaming of what flights?

★

News Hawker

Boston
> *Now!*
Boston
> *Now!*
When I say,
> "Boston,"
you say,
> "Now."

Metro ain't doin' it,
Boston Now IS.

Givin' away
one thousand dollars
every week!

Is that too much money?
You don't want my paper?
OK.
Don't take it!

Boston
> *Now!*
Boston

Now!
When I say,
    "Boston,"
you say,
    "Now."

Calendar Pages 2012

January

Banked snow, waist-high at subway entrance,
now rheumy and shrinking in January thaw
to reveal the chrome handlebars and green painted frame
of this entombed bicycle stenciled with black letters:
"15 SPEEDS."

★

March

Blue Chevy pickup, parked on bare asphalt,
with yellow plow still fixed to its prow,
facing a mound of snow, once pristine,
but now melt-pocked, soot-stained,
and topped with a crude wooden sign
that someone hand-lettered in good humor:
"FREE SNOW!"

★

October

Along the granite lintel of a second story window
in the brick wall of a schoolhouse facing the train tracks,
some child has scrawled with black paint,
"MESSIAH COMING SOON."

Three of a Kind

1. For John Wieners, in memoriam

Small iron grated windows,
kept for authenticity,
high in the massive granite façade
of renovated Charles Street Jail,
now open under new management
as the Liberty Hotel.

White Hummer stretch limousine
parked at curbside;
business-suited men, women
in high heels and cocktail dresses
lined up, awaiting admission
to the Clink restaurant, the Alibi Bar.

2. Corner of Bond & Pacific
       For Robert Hershon
       "You call that a neighborhood?"

Solitary tree in curbside plot,
brick sidewalk surrounding,
keeping company with
bottle caps, glass shards,
sodden paper napkins,
Dunkin' Donuts coffee cups. . . .

Sign affixed to its trunk,
stamped with official borough seal
and protected against the elements
by a plastic sleeve, proclaims:
"GREENEST BLOCK IN BROOKLYN."

3. *Homage*
>   Mount Auburn Cemetery, Cambridge

Planted at the intersection
of Tulip and Orchis lanes,
among granite obelisks, mausoleums,
ornate statuary,
this plain, rectangular, gray stone
inscribed with just name & dates:

ROBERT CREELEY
MAY 21, 1926–
MARCH 29, 2005

Evergreen wreath
laid at its foot,
two small skipping stones
placed, one at each
corner on the top
by some hand, in a
private gesture of homage.

En Route

1 *Red Line Riddle* (Boston)

Coed on subway platform
swigging OJ from a carton:

knee-high black leather boots,
black leather short-shorts and halter-top,

hooded black face-mask
with pointy ears sticking up.

Costume? What occasion?
Ah, *METRO'S* got the answer:

"DARK KNIGHT.
Premiere today."

2. (Somerville)

Outside
Eglise Baptiste de la Bible
a formerly Catholic
neighborhood church
now Haitian Baptist

a signboard proclaims:
HELL IS REAL—
Sunday's sermon
in foot-high letters.

Added in italics beneath
 (an attempt at outreach?)
New!
English Translation!

3. *A–Train Riddle* (Manhattan)

Eyes drawn to
gilt-flecked lettering
on the black tee-shirt

of the brown-skinned,
middle-aged woman
seated across the aisle.

Keeping Jesus Strong, 1611–2011
printed above the silk-screened image
of an open book.

Below, another cryptic caption:
400 Years, Keeping Jesus Strong,
variation on the same puzzling theme.

Wait! Got it!
400th anniversary
of the King James Bible!

4. Sunday Morning (Brooklyn)

Only two storefronts
on this side-street
not shuttered.

Outside one
a sandwich board
on the sidewalk

(black print,
all caps)
advertises

SHOE REPAIR
CUT KEYS
CASH 4 GOLD

The other
three doors down:
signboard

written in cursive
with blue Magic Marker,
invites:

LOST LIT?
COME BE FOUND!
WRITING WORKSHOP.

Who said poetry
and commerce
can't mix?

Calendar Pages 2012/2013

You can observe a lot just by watching.
—Yogi Berra

August

Two men in business suits
        step off the homebound train.
                First one, then the other,
loosens his necktie.

⋆

September

Although missing handlebars,
        seat, and both wheels,
                a bicycle nevertheless
securely chained to this lamppost.

⋆

October

Startled to see reflected
        in the darkened window
                of this rush hour train entering a tunnel
my beard so white.

⋆

November

The neighbor's young wife
     out early in pajamas and slippers
          shivering in her husband's overcoat
walking the dog.

★

December

Snowman in a neighbor's front yard:
     felt hat, plaid muffler,
          red wool mittens,
and yellow gaiters where some dog peed.

★

January

Having departed the bus in a squall,
     a hooded sweatshirt and an umbrella,
          arm in arm, laughing,
navigate snowdrifts together.

★

February (Valentine's Day)

Inside: porcelain-skin mannequins
     in skimpy, red bikinis.
Outside: shoppers in drab wool coats,
     collars turned up.

Flâneuries: Harvard Square

Morning commuters in a hurry
pay no mind—or do they?—
to three sleepers in stocking feet
stretched out on benches,
a pair of shoes tucked neatly beneath each.

Early shoppers streaming by.
Two homeless teens, a girl and her beau,
seated cross-legged on a waist-high brick wall

each cradling a marker-scribbled sign:
Hers (sarcastic?): *Will Take Verbal Abuse (for) $1.00*
His (confrontational): *Fuck You. Pay Me.*

On a bench at the crosswalk,
an elderly woman in housedress,
babushka and slippers,
stockingless, varicose calves—
a widow? a pensioner? both?

A sign, hanging
on the walker parked next to her:
TREAT A GRANNY TO BRUNCH—
How to read this: lighthearted? ironic?

No ambiguity here: young man
seated on pavement at the subway entrance,
sound asleep, back pressed against kiosk,
chin on knees. Propped against his legs

a block-lettered cardboard sign:
WILL SOMEONE, PLEASE,
SPARE A FEW DOLLARS
SO I CAN BE ANYPLACE BUT HERE!
Panhandler: but no paper cup, no upturned cap: novice?

Approaching from up the avenue
a couple in matching leather jackets
(tourists? locals out for a brisk stroll?)
with matching French poodles on short leashes.
(Who's leading who?)

The balding black sidewalk hawker
turns as they pass
calls after them:
"Spare Change newspaper.
One dollar.
One dollar, *Spare Change!"*

Smoking under office building eaves,
two women—secretaries?— overheard jawing.
One nods in the direction of a sleeping drunk:
"You know how to tell when an alcoholic
has hit rock bottom?" (a joke?)

"No," replies the other, ash end
of her cigarette drooping "Tell me."
"When you catch him sipping vanilla extract."
punch line or hard-won knowledge?

Many questions, few answers.

II. Pine Pillow Book

Things That Gain by Being Painted: Pines. Autumn fields. Mountain villages and paths. Cranes and deer. A very cold winter scene; an unspeakably hot summer scene.

—Sei Shōnagon, *The Pillow Book*

Pine Pillow Book

The area is particularly fascinating to inlanders,
because both the villages and the people have
distinctive characteristics, developed by long contact
with the sea.
—WPA Guide, *The Pine Tree State,* ca. 1936

27:VII:2013

Two signs at the crest of County Road:
SUNSET CAMPGROUND & RV PARK,
followed by:
SUNRISE BAY & QUODDY VIEW APARTMENTS.

Each advertised as the "easternmost" of its kind
(as in easternmost potter, quilter, library, tavern, lighthouse . . .).

> *Welcome to Lubec.*
> *The Easternmost Town in the U.S.*
> *Est. 1811*

Just past the turnout to Monica's Gourmet Chocolats,
a sign pointing right, advertising "Fitness Center, ¼ mile."

Ah! No-guilt vacation!

★

Roadside cemetery's white marble stones—
a few listing, but most upright—
all afflicted with rashes of orange lichen.
Chiseled on one, the epitaph:

"Here lies one Wood,
Encased in wood.
One Wood within another.
The outer wood is very good,
We cannot praise the other."

28:VII:2013

V of ducks passing overhead:
door hinges   [no break]
creaking open, closed.

Jet plane high up,
its four white tines
silently raking the cloudless blue.

Hummingbird downshifting mid-air,
abruptly stopping
on its metaphorical dime.

Yellow jackets nectaring in a patch of jewelweed:
pickpockets
working an outdoor concert crowd.

29:VII:2013

For Rent: "Whale of a View Cottage."

★

Swallowed, one after the other:
trees, shingled cottages, rocky head.
Bulimic fog later, disgorging them—
headland, cottages, trees— in reverse order.

Soiled, ragged-edge clouds
hang from an invisible clothesline,
stretching to the horizon.

Tide slowly drawing back the sheet,
exposing the ribs and backbone
of a sunken dory.

★

Terns on a spit of strand:
Common terns? Roseate terns? No, neither!
Arctic terns lifting off, landing, lifting off again,
one after another, after another—
never mind air-traffic control.
(What's that pun? Leave no tern un-stoned.)

★

"Seaview Rest Home: Vacancy"

30:VII:2013

"Bold" Coast Idyll

So much depends upon this lobster boat
anchored between islands sporting piney crowns,
too small for habitation,
each no bigger than the boat itself.

Gentle breezes, dimpling the bay;
incoming tide nibbling the pebbled shore.

★

Not wasps: bees;
bumblebees not yellow jackets
nuzzled deep
in jewelweed horns:

fluted, orange skirts
snugly fitted
around fat black bellies;

bobbing as one
on slender, green threads:
bees and blossoms.

   ★

Hen-of-the-woods, chicken-of-the-woods, old-man-of-the-woods;
    turkey-tail, fairy cup, witches' butter.

Not tipler's bane, lawyer's wig (a.k.a. shaggy mane);
monarch, not viceroy; *mourning,* not morning cloak.

Black Point, Sandy Point, Long Point, Otter Point;
Fairy Head, Eastern Nubble, "Bold" Coast.

   ★

Lazing on rocky beach,
book open on lap,
my only companion
all afternoon, the sea,
shuffling its deck of cards.

Idyll, not idle.

1:VIII–6:VIII:2013

Eastport Suite

Loud belch and gurgle
of diesel boat motor turning over:
the working harbor's cockcrow at 3:45 a.m.

Later, a delivery truck idling outside
Dastardly Dick's "Wicked Good" Coffee Shop;
strains of Neil Young from its radio.

Still later: hammering, pneumatic riveting,
metal clanking against hollow metal,
whine of an electric winch lowering traps.

Dim headlights of a pickup truck on wharf,
the only thing visible in fog
the consistency of Campbell's cream of mushroom soup.

Gulls, heard but not seen,
guffawing, yucking it up.

   ★

Sunday services over, fog burning off, tide turned,
cars, trucks pulling up, parking on the fish pier;

standing before each
a man with fishing pole, casting.

"Whatcha catchin'?"
"Mackerel, if they'd bite."

★

Classified:
"WICKED SUMMER SALE: Koozies and drink holders in stock, Mackerel lures, lots to choose from, clams and crawlers for bait, sinkers, swivels, monofilament and handlining frames. Pick up a free tide chart while you're here. Moose Island Marine, at the breakwater, Eastport."

★

With slow wing-strokes,
a gull emerges out of fog,
then is swallowed again.

Just a rumor of buildings
that car tires whisper in passing.

Here, a granite cornice;
there, a streetlight's gooseneck.

Here, a brick chimney;
there, a ship's mast top.

Then, swallowed in fog again.

★

Rusting, corrugated-metal Quonset hut,
perched on a fenced-off, badly listing pier—
abandoned? Condemned?—

    R.D. HOBBS
    C-FOOD

50

in faded red letters
on a dingy white background;

below, in block letters,
a few obscured, erased:

SEA   CHINS

SCALL   IMP

OBSTERS

Time-capsule from a bygone era: cryptic.

    ★

Q: What do you call a sardine packer?
A: Herring choker.

Not sardines, *herring*;
juvenile Atlantic herring (*Clupea harengus),*
not European pilchard (*Sardina pilchardus*):
salted, smoked, pickled, and canned.

Red Hen, Blue Horse, Possum—Eastport brands;
Stag, Mellon, Leader, Columbian—Lubec.

"Little fish biled in ile."

Seacoast Canning, Columbian Canning, Mawhinney & Ramsdell,
Lubec Sardine, American Can, North Lubec Manufacturing and
Canning—
gone, all long gone.

    ★

Late model Chevy hatchback,
parked in the yard of a boarded-up house,
tall weeds grown up around it.

Florets of rust on chassis and fenders;
tailgate pocked with dime-size holes,
where some sportsman took target practice.

★

Water Street

I want you to love me like my dog does, honey.
He never says 'I wish you made more money.'

Cowboy music spilling from the takeout window
at Atlantic House Coffee and Deli:

I want you to love me like my dog does, baby.
He never tells me that he's sick of this house.
He never says why don't you get off that couch?

★

State Police Blotter, *Quoddy Tides*:

"On July 19 Trooper Andrew Foss handled a bad check complaint in
Pembroke where Adam Farley, 33, was summonsed for negotiating a
worthless instrument."

"On August 1 Sgt. Jeffrey Ingemi handled a criminal mischief complaint
in Lubec, where a mailbox was damaged for a second time. Four local
juveniles admitted to the damage, paid for the last time they pulled it

out of the ground, dug a new hole for the new mailbox they bought, and are going to church for a couple of weeks with the victim at the victim's request."

★

What better alarm clock
than a buzz-saw
missing its off-switch?

What better alarm clock
than an aluminum extension ladder
going up, coming down, going back up again?

What better alarm clock
than a forklift backing up
the entire length of the fish pier?

What better alarm clock than a delivery truck,
idling the duration of a lumberjack breakfast
with an extra side of pancakes?

What better alarm clock
than a chain-saw
cutting cordwood to last through the next Ice Age?

★

Eastport Pirate Festival flier:
Pirate parade
Pirate ball
Pirate sail
Pirate bed races
(I thought they slept in hammocks.)

Pirate invasion
Pirate encampment
Pirate reenactment
Cannon battles
(Really?)

Thieves market
(Is that like a yard sale?)

The largest Pirate Festival in New England
(How many can there be?)

Costumes strongly recommended.
(Or else what? The gangplank?)

★

> *"Smuggling was rampant . . . sugar, molasses, flour, and rum. . . .*
> *Any night innkeepers might be awakened by furtive knocks on their*
> *doors. . . . one tavern keeper had a special room for deserting British*
> *sailors whom he recognized by their sea-soaked clothing, for they usually*
> *swam ashore."*
>
> —WPA Guide, *The Pine Tree State,* ca. 1936

7:VIII:2013

Passamaquoddy: "pollock plenty place."

Campobello: "beautiful meadow,"

★

54

Bare concrete slab with PVC pipes sticking up,
freshly mown grassy field surrounding; lot vacant
but for two shiny green John Deere tractors
parked side-by-each.

Small array of dish antennae
point skyward on a fog-damp lawn:
spiders seeking signs of arachnid intelligence
beyond the Milky Way.

Tree trunks stripped of bark and limbs,
stacked lengthwise in a field:
their sun-bleached silver patina.

In a different field, two white cabin cruisers up on blocks
motionless in a sea of tall undulating grasses.

Rusted-out GMC dump truck abandoned in yet another field:
its bullet-constellated windshield.

8:VIII:2013

Dories with their snaking painters
rest on the sandy, damp bottom
of Carrying Way Cove
at lowest of low tides.

High and dry, two lobster boats
list on their keels; a third
with wire traps stacked precariously high
at lowest of low tides.

Weed-draped rocky ridges,
      stubble of gone pilings,
          shreds of green netting,
              frayed hanks of nylon rope . . .
exposed by this lowest of low tides.

9:VIII:2013

"*Devil's paintbrush grows in profusion, spreading through the fields to
the grief of the farmer and the joy of the passer-by.*"
      —WPA Guide, *The Pine Tree State,* ca. 1936

Tansy, mullein, chicory, yarrow;
lady's thumb, bachelor's button, Indian paintbrush . . .
not weeds, wildflowers;
wildflowers not weeds.

Foghorn blasting the announcement
that festivities are about to commence
in the lawn spider pavilions
decorated with crystal globes.

Green frog seated on roadside gravel,
having safely negotiated the busy county two-lane,
now contemplating the muddy drainage ditch
yawning before him.

Ruby-throated hummingbird pulls up abruptly
before beach roses fronting porch, where I sit,
newspaper open on my lap,
eyeing him eyeing me eyeing him;
then—zip—gone.

10:VIII:2013

Huckleberry bog or maritime forest, what's your preference?
Cedar fen or tall grass meadow? Sheer cliffs or chalky bluffs?
Outcrops or inlets; cobble beaches or rocky headlands?

What say we slog through peatland seeps over riprap trails and split-log
boardwalks from Carrying Place Cove to Quoddy Head Heath? We'll
search for crowberry blues (they're rare butterflies) and carnivorous
pitcher plants. Along the way we can feast our eyes on deer-hair sedge,
baked-apple berry, and creeping juniper.

Then let's backtrack, cross Dump Road, and hike to Hamilton Cove,
enjoying the meadowsweet meadowlands, the speckled alder and
Labrador tea barren, crossing the bog where Canada bluejoint and
sphagnum moss give way to dry rocky outcroppings sporting three-
toothed cinquefoil.

We'll pass from red-maple lowlands to fir and spruce highlands. There
we can bivouac with just our rucksacks on the barren xeric overlook
surrounded by patches of hydric vegetation with the crashing Atlantic
far below.

11:VIII:2013

Summer gale,
        empty chairs
                on neighboring cottage porch,
rocking.

                ★

Surf crawling up the strand.
>Shorebirds scurry ahead of it,
>>then turn abruptly at the berm
to chase it back down.

★

Foghorn's fanfare—
>*Huzzah, huzzah—*
>>announcing this crone pine's emergence
from fog and sea mist.

★

The woodsman
>his swarm of gnats;
the lobster boat
>its cloud of gulls.

★

A spider's gossamer sail
>rigged between porch rails,
>>billowing
in the summer breeze.

★

Dog days of summer:
>a girl and her reflection
>>walking slowly together
along marsh pond's edge.

★

House at marsh pond's edge
       joined to its mirror image—
              who's to say
which is right-side up?

12:VIII:2013

Classified: "Pine needle-stuffed pillows for sale."

★

Downeast Coastal News:

"Backyard Beekeepers Buzz Up A Swarm of Pollination, Honey."

"Blackfly Ball Organizers Feel Sting of Criticism."

"Driver Swerves to Avoid Moose, Hits Bear Instead."

III. Natural Histories

To the natural philosopher there is no ... object unimportant or trifling . . . a soap bubble . . . an apple . . . a pebble . . . He walks in the midst of wonders.

–John Herschel

How wonderful to write with a small pen: the recovery of precision.

—Theodore Roethke, *Notebooks*

Admonitions

Only that day dawns to which we are awake.
—Henry David Thoreau

1.

You stand on the pedestrian median between lanes of traffic,
waiting for the walk light,

gazing down to where rain has washed up
winged seeds, flotsam of sodden leaf-litter,

the butt ends of cigarettes, crushed under heels . . .
paying no mind to the chicory sprout

that has put on, just for you,
this display of pinwheel petals

under an echoing blue sky,
with not a single cloud in sight.

2.

Lift your eyes from the gutter —Yes, you! —
and behold this pastel-colored–Easter-egg sky

with jagged line of white light
streaming through the crack in its shell.

3.

Go ahead.
Be astonished

by this Zen painting
framed in your window:

the flowering pear tree's
network of branches—

bold black brush strokes—
surrounded by clouds of white petals.

4.

Chicory sprouting in the crack
between curb and sidewalk,
its petals now pursed
against this summer drizzle—

why do you spurn the praises
of friends and strangers alike?

5.

Mist rises in coiled cornrows
from the surface of Fresh Pond;

sun just peeking over the tree line,
not a breath of wind to rustle leaves—

how many more sleepless nights
can you endure?

6.

Where the turnpike threads
through blasted bedrock—

Look up!
Look up from your book—

Take note of the ancient rock faces
with snow-crested brows!

Observe the blue-ice beards,
the silver-gray dreadlocks.

7.

Waste lot bordering
abandoned harbor-side pump house:

This used to be real estate,
as in the Talking Heads' song,
Now it's only fields and trees.

Where clover, sumac, elephant grass;
where pheasants, wild turkey, field mice and rabbits;

where, in milkweed patches,
Mexico bound monarchs down from the Maritimes . . .

now bulldozers scrape bare and level the earth
to put up a parking lot!

Don't it always seem to go
That you don't know what you've got
till it's gone?

8.

This ornamental cherry tree
the city planted at curbside

today is a branched candelabra
tricked out in flames

as in the Shaker painting "Blazing Tree":
each wick of leaf is burning

bright autumnal orange,
a gift to us

homeward bound commuters
on the 73 bus, stalled in traffic —

Mother Ann
would've approved.

After Utamaro's *Chorus of Birds and Insects*

> *. . . not to disclose the timeless, but to discern the transient,*
> *to clasp the texture of experience—a passing moment, an*
> *instant's glimpse, a sensation . . .*
> —Edward Rothstein, on the aesthetic of *Ehon*
> (Japanese artist books).

Panel 1

Bordering train tracks,
an undulating green sea

of weeds and tall grasses,
with flecks of white foam—

Queen Ann's lace—
at the wave crests.

Panel 2

Oak leaves pressed to black asphalt
in a decorative motif

ring this puddle in which
three sparrows ruffling feathers

plash excitedly:
Cheep! Cheep! Cheep!

Panel 3

Mold-mottled grape leaves
on backyard trellis

formally arrayed as in
wallpaper designs by William Morris —

curly tendrils and crisscrossed vines
showing through, on which perch

plump sparrows testing
pendent fruit's ripeness.

Panel 4

Hydrangea blossoms opened and opening:
this one blue, that one pink, another magenta;

petals slowly bruising from the edges inward
toward creamy white centers

on every nodding stalk but this
one that pruning shears missed

on which still hang last season's
rust-stained crinolines.

Panel 5

Ink-black thumb smudges
on otherwise white fur,

this crouching cat,
muscles tensed,

balanced atop
chain-link fence

face to face with
gray squirrel, its tail erect—

two trains on a collision course—
fur soon to fly.

Panel 6

A carpet of bluebells, spread
beneath forsythia's golden crown,

whose bowed branches so recently
bore the weight of new fallen snow.

Along the grape arbor,
blackheads have erupted

along the blistered skin
of last season's vines.

Panel 7

In the thorny tangle
of trellised bramble roses,

a trio of squabbling sparrows
squawk, peck, bat their wings.

Neighborhood tabby,
the only other spectator,

squatting on matted grass beneath,
casts a knowing glance in my direction.

Panel 8

Ancient backyard cedar,
whose tippy-top tickles the clouds,

today rocks back and forth in wide arcs
animated by a sudden gale.

Its boughs lift and fall,
lift, fall, and sway, side to side,

in ripples of carnival-fat-lady belly laughter
while droplets from the darkened sky

strike my upturned face,
speckle my eyeglasses.

Panel 9

Brother squirrel
perched on haunches,

nibbling the edges
of a just-plucked mushroom

can't you hear
my empty stomach grumble?

Panel 10

Not the grackle feathers
splayed in a fan, bottom-side up,

on flattened backyard grass
(which, ahem, needs mowing)

left as a 'present'
by neighbor Reneé's white Turkish cat

but rather this moth, *Catocala innubens,*
expired, belly up,

just inside my front porch door —
itself a gift:

underwings showing to advantage
the concentric bands,

jack-o-lantern orange
alternating with brown velvet,

signature of its family,
hence the name *beautiful below.*

Panel 11: Envoy

Seated under grape arbor
with notebook open

like old Fabre
at his *harmas* at Serinan,

"Setting down
 the days."

Here, too,
"The common wasp

and the *Polistes*
are my dinner guests."

Right now,
"They visit my table

to see if the grapes served
are as ripe as they look."

Natural Histories

Nature will bear the closest inspection. She invites us to lay our eye level with her smallest leaf, and take an insect view of its plain.
—Henry David Thoreau

Fly on windowsill
wringing its hands—
are fly worries
fly-size?

★

Windfall apples and overripe grapes
litter my patio;
drunken wasps
staggering amid the bounty.

★

Neighborhood tabby
seated on haunches, forepaw extended,
sparring with white butterfly:
Felis catus vs. *Pieris rapae.*

★

As Jack his beanstalk,
the snail, this sunflower.
The fighter pilot, his carrier deck;
the dragonfly, this grass blade.

★

Frenzied swarm of starlings
flying hither, thither; thither, hither;
mindful neither of where they are headed
nor what they are looking for.

★

The neighbor's busy cat
enters, exits; re-enters, re-exists
all afternoon by way of the screen door
left open a crack.

★

Tiny brown ant
climbs up my bare calf;
not finding what it was seeking,
retraces its path.

★

Breathless afternoon:
bees nectaring, wasps burrowing,
white butterfly waltzing
among blue and purple hydrangeas.

★

Impatient ants,
intoxicated by the fragrance
of peony buds not yet opened,
trying to pry apart the petals.

★

Cobwebs cover
my backyard grill.
Webs empty, grill cold,
spiders and me both hungry.

★

Rain all afternoon;
now, this cloudless night:
cat lapping stars in backyard puddle,
sparrows bathing on trashcan lid.

★

Lacking bridesmaids,
the garden slug
drags her own silk train
down this moonlit path.

★

Full summer moon
resting atop the high wooden fence
that separates neighbor from neighbor:
Thee from Me; Me from Thee.

★

Starless night,
dinner guest departed,
lighted lantern on patio table,
moths to keep me company.

Passer domesticus

. . . deliciae meae puellae—Catullus 2

Perched outside my window
on an ice-glazed limb
two plump sparrows without necks,
waiting out winter.

★

Among all the birds at my feeder
only sparrows come to dine,
wearing clean bibs
tucked into their collars.

★

Not the downy woodpecker,
but rather sparrows woke me,
tapping at my window to complain
that the feeder's empty.

★

Sparrows mid-air, fluttering wings,
waiting in a holding pattern
for a turn at the feeder:
Passer domesticus traffic control.

★

Pull up the sheet, cover your nakedness!
No, it isn't the neighbor,
smoking outside again on his back porch;
it's sparrows on the windowsill, gawking.

★

One, two, three, four, five,
six sparrows crowding my feeder;
six versions
of the same poem.

Cupid's Dart[1]

I'd like to give my gardening girlfriend a bouquet of flower
seeds that have love in their names for Valentine's Day. . . .
If this is possible, please suggest things to look for. . . .
—Garden Q & A, New York Times

Slender Naiad[2]
Love-in-idleness[3]
Kiss-me-over-the-garden-gate[4]

Lady's Maid[5]
Heart's Delight[6]
Kiss-me-quick[7]

Love-in-a-mist[8]
None-so-pretty[9]
Kiss-me-over-the-garden-gate

Love-in-a-puff[10]
Night sensation[11]
Kiss-me-quick

Sleeping beauty[12]
Cupid's dart
Love-lies-bleeding[13]
Red-hot poker[14]
Love-lies-bleeding

Small Alison[15]
Lad's love[16]
Forget-me-not[17]

Sweet Nancy[18]
Eternal flame[19]
Love–lies–bleeding

Bouncing Bet[20]
Black–eyed Susan[21]
Busy Lizzie[22]
Forget–me–not
Fair maids of February[23]
Forget–me–not

1. *Catanache caerulea*; 2. *Najas flexilis* (English); 3. *Viola tricolo*;
4. *Polygonum orientale*; 5. *Artemisia chamaemelifolia* (various);
6. *Abronia fragrans* (North America); 7. *Brunfelsia latifolia* (various);
8. *Nigella damascena*; 9. *Silene armeria* (United States);
10. *Cardiospermum halicacabum*; 11. *Polianthes tuberosa* (English);
12. Oxalis montana (English); 13. *Amaranthus caudatus*;
14. *Kniphofia uvaria*; 15. *Alyssum alyssoides* (United States);
16. *Artemisia abrotanum*; 17. *Myosotis verna*; 18. *Achillea ageratum*
(English); 19. *Calathea crocata*); 20. *Saponaria officinalis*;
21. *Thunbergia alata*; 22. *Impatiens walleriana*; 23. *Galanthus nivalis*
(various).

Audubon Calendar

January

Gathered in a circle
on the frozen river:
gulls loudly celebrating
a patch of open water.

★

February

Retracing my steps in a snowsquall
after putting out trash
my footprints
have already vanished.

★

March

Sunny morning, eaves dripping,
roof-sloughed snow's
thud
in the yard below.

★

April

4 a.m. dark, wide awake.
Why?
Oh, listen!
Cardinal has returned.

★

May

In the freshly turned garden,
yesterday's boot print
brimming with rainwater
in which a slug has drowned.

★

June
Backyard pigeons
doing lazy laps all afternoon:
garage roof to porch gutter,
porch gutter to garage roof.

★

July

Between my neighbors' porch and backyard cedar,
a squirrel practices tightrope walking
along the clothesline draped with
damp white briefs, pastel panties.

★

August

Windows open wide,
but no hint of breeze;
sleepless under a thin sheet,
sand between my toes.

★

September

Inchworm with head in air,
clinging to the end of a stalk by just its hind legs,
unable to advance,
but unwilling to back down.

★

October

Hiking in a grove
of towering white pines
planted in another century
my posture has improved.

★

November

Dusting of new snow in yard,
unblemished, but for pawprints—
a trail that ends
directly beneath the birdfeeder.

★

December

Deep in a suburban wood,
skiing at dusk with snow falling,
the only sound
my own deep breathing.

IV. Go to the Pine:
Quoddy Journals 2005–2010

Go to the pine if you want to learn about pine. . . .
—Basho

"Bold Coast" Partita: Chaconne

[Slow Dance, Repeated Harmonic Pattern]

Pink garden hostas'
rain–damp
pendent blossoms

sway
on tall stalks
to foghorn's tune,

a single droplet
at each tip,
glistening.

Quoddy Journal I (2005)

> *I should recommend . . . keeping . . . a small*
> *memorandum-book in the breast-pocket, with its*
> *well-cut sheathed pencil, ready for notes on passing*
> *opportunities.*
>
> —John Ruskin, *The Elements of Drawing*

31:VII:05

White-haired, middle-aged woman dressed in black jersey, black jeans, black rubber boots, combing among stubbly pilings of a gone Eastport wharf at low tide, her yellow Labrador retriever leading the way. Aged dragger moored to rusty red buoy off-shore; hull, drab green; cabin, white—both badly in need of fresh paint. Lone sailboat plying wind-riffled waters of the bay: white hull, white mast, puffed white jib. Boxy houses, white-sided with black roofs, (but for one roof that's brick red), perch on stilts on rocky ledges up and down the shore. Farther east Camp(o)bell(o) Island, a furzy line drawn with sprucy-gray crayon; silvery arch of the International Bridge, Bay of Fundy beyond.

1:VIII:05

Steep trails
lead down sheer cliffs
past sea-eroded caves,
to sandless beaches
with high berms of heaped,
sea-smoothed, egg-shaped rocks
where when the tide goes out,
the tide goes out
& out & out,
and you pick your barefoot way
along the "ocean bottom."

★

2:VIII:05

Window looking out onto tidal marsh, sandbar and beach bordering this reach of Passamaquoddy Bay. Campobello beyond, Grand Manan beyond that.

Cool mist blows in over Quoddy Head, followed by heavy fog that partially, then fully enshrouds all. Foghorn counsels, "Sleep. Sleep." And I do. Soundly.

★

3:VIII:05

Sun's broken yolk
streaking the horizon
blood-orange.

★

4:VIII:05

Diorama placard at Calais Museum reads: "*Passamaquoddy*: People of
　　the Dawn."
Greet the dawn is what I do each day. Does that qualify for honorary
　　tribal status?

★

5:VIII:05

Fickle butterfly
(yellow sulfur)
settles on purple clover,
momentarily,
then flits off to visit
the next flower head.
Startled grasshoppers
leap up from tall grass,
wings a-whir.
Lone crow pushes off from fir bough,
strokes the damp air—
rower putting his back into it,
surveying the salt marsh
end to end.

★

6:VIII:05

Preserved between pages
of last summer's
spiral notebook:

> *Mt. Tom*
> *SIX BY FOUR*
> 80 Sheets
> *Narrow Ruled*
> *Bob Slate Stationer*
> Cambridge, Mass.

One yellow cinquefoil,
pressed, dried,
suitable for framing.

★

7:VIII:05

Coming over rise
upon apparition:
deer in the road,
wide-eyed, quizzical—
doe & me both.

Then blink-of-an-eye gone.
(Who blinked first?)
Fog. Fog in headlights.

★

9:VIII:05

Stop in at Jim Blankman's Eastport woodworking shop. He *Restores Woodies, Builds Woodie Teardrop Trailers, Luthier* [What's a luthier?], *Crafts Scooters, Skateboards and Luges." Admire some of his custom-designed, handcrafted ash boxes and wooden coffins.*

Just imagine yourself laid out in a finely crafted pine box with wooden handles, lined with the fabric of your choice. How about this one lined in a favorite, hunter's red plaid flannel. Various shades of satin are also used. The fabric design choices are yours. The price for this coffin is about $500 [A bargain as coffins go]. *Metal handles and more elaborate fabrics are available at an extra charge* [But of course]. *Shipping can be arranged throughout the United States* [How convenient].

Check out this other coffin, *finely crafted to closely resemble the Woodies that Jim lovingly restores. Notice the detail in the inner top, the leather outer top, the metal work, and the fine woods. Shipping can be arranged throughout the United States.* [But of course.]

★

10:VIII:05

Sun–bleached, salt air weathered,
lichen–crusted, wooden lawn chair,
overlooking salt marsh, bay,
and distant headlands,
where I sit taking inventory of my realm:
beach peas, beach roses, beach burdocks,
& sea lavender. Field at my back
grown up with cow vetch, butter-and-eggs,
wild daisy, goldenrod,
purple and white clover,
Queen Ann's lace . . .

★

11:VIII:05

Moonless dark
enveloping
road, fields, marsh,
and bay beyond.

House dark too
but for one
lighted room:

Gianni
blowing his sax.
Coyote chorus
across the road
chimes in:

"They Can't
Take That
Away
From Me."

★

12:VIII:05

The fisher is a fearless predator—or so I've read (*Britannica*, 1955
edition). Will face off with a porcupine, snapping at the animal's snout
until it goes into shock; then will roll the body over to get at its soft
underbelly. Evidence: empty sack of quills in roadside ditch.

★

13:VIII:05

Cormorants
perched on rocks,
noses in the air,
are not so
disinterested
as they may seem,
Bream.

Sister cormorant
trolls nearby
periscope up
against the in-
coming tide

★

14:VIII:05

Sign posted on the lawn: "Cottage for Sale."
Its name painted over the front door: *Dontwantaquitit.*

★

15:VIII:05

Crystal clear air this 5 AM is a parting gift. Just two bands of Crayola-color burnt-orange cloud, illuminated by the not-yet-peeking-over-the-horizon sun. Lone lobster boat in the distance, plying the water between dark landmasses, heading for open sea. White clapboard and red roof houses on Quoddy Head cleanly etched by the gathering light. Picture postcard perfect!

"Bold Coast" Partita: Allemande

[Stately Dance in Duple Meter or Lively Dance in Triple Meter]

Pastoral signboard
outside white clapboard Baptist church
on Coastal Route 1 North
counsels:
       "Bad Economy
       Invest in Faith"

Quoddy Journal II (2006)

I just had to jot down these fleeting things . . .
a rapid notation in watercolor and pencil: an informal
daubing of contrasting colors, tones, and hues.
— Henri-Edmond Cross, French painter
(1856 –1910).

23:VII:06

Young woman enters office of the Mollynocket Motel, seeking a room for beau and self. This in West Paris, Maine, just north of Poland and Norway, east of Sweden and Denmark, but south of Peru and Mexico, Maine. Manager seated at the desk looks up, takes her measure, notices the glitter-flecked letters blazoned across her tee shirt:
"New . . . York . . . City," he exclaims, emphasizing each word.
"No," she replies. "I ain't *from* there . . . But I been there."

★

24:VII:06

Constellations of dew
on window screens.
Spider, suspended
on invisible filaments just outside,
stages a tap dance
to foghorn accompaniment.
Cha-cha. Cha. Cha. Cha.

★

97

25:VII:06

Slate-gray cloudbank drawn across horizon.
Newly risen sun winking at its scalloped edge.

★

26:VII:06

Bangor Daily News:
"The Brady Gang came to Maine in the fall of 1937 for the same reasons
21st century criminals venture north of Boston—seafood, foliage, and
guns."
Guns? Ah, guns!

PAWN
GUNZ
GUNSHOP
AHEAD

★

27:VII:06
Watercolor

Dull pewter morning sky;
oilcloth spread over harbor,
tucked in at shoreline,
set with salt and pepper shaker buoys
beside toy boats painted primary colors;
humpbacked island at harbor's mouth
in the shape of an overturned ladle.

Washboard ripples
fill the narrow channel
between shore and the island
with its comb of firs.

Chicken-wire fence
edges weed-wigged rocks
bordering a field
where sheep graze,
while sparrows and starlings
hop and peck among
clumps of close-cropped grass
peppered with droppings.

Screeching gulls strafe the yard,
then settle on the slouching,
lichen-crusted chicken coop's
tarpaper roof. One fidgets,
tucks its wings, fixes its flinty gaze
on the paint-flaked dory turned turtle.

★

28:VII:06

. . . *violation of scallop rule, $250*
. . . *hand fishing sea urchin without license, $500*
. . . *negotiating worthless instrument, $150*
. . . *violation of marine worm rule, $250*
. . .*failing to kindle in prudent manner, $100*
      – Machias District court cases, *Bangor Daily News*

★

29:VII:06

Between the muddy banks
of this narrow inlet
fringed with damp grasses,
the sea twice daily
insinuates its tongue.

★

30:VII:06

Sudden wind beneath
a darkening sky
raises waves in orderly ranks
to charge the shore.

Shudders ripple through cattails
rooted in a ditch;
pelting rain follows,
bending them double.

Sky now brightening,
a lone gull, sporting white hood,
gray cape, yellow leggings,
stalks field and shoreline
to assess the carnage.

★

31:VII:06

Field Note: *Sturnus vulgarus* [the common starling]

Little old men out of 19th Century Russian novels
(Goncharov? Gogol?),
wearing dark, ash-flecked greatcoats,
pace the length and breadth of this yard.

Bent at the waist, heads down,
hands folded behind backs, they search,
among grass blades and sheep droppings,
for lost thoughts.

★

1:VIII:06

Road Sign:
EWESFUL ITEMS

★

2:VIII:06

Fisherman in muck-crusted waders
stacking traps on the wharf,
greasy-haired, unshaven, grimy with sweat,
stands stock still, eyes fixed
on the candy-apple-red-painted toenails
of a woman in Bermuda shorts,

transacting a purchase
of lobsters for her dinner.

★

3:VIII:06

No remnant of the customhouse
at Customhouse Beach,
but countless multicolored,
sea-worn, sea-smoothed
glass and pottery shards.

Also one rust-crusted
 V-6 engine block,
minus pistons, rods,
manifolds, et cetera—

object of fascination
to my teenage son
experiencing nostalgia
for a past he never knew.

★

5:VIII:06
5 AM Sacramental Landscape

Old Testament night
of thunder, lightning, hail,
and biblical downpours.

Now dawn arrives,

startling as the risen Christ
in Grünewald's painting, "The Resurrection."

Spread out across the bay,
a shimmering golden platter
rests on white muslin,

reflection of the dazzling
eucharistic orb now suspended
an arm's-length above the horizon.

★

6:VIII:06
With apologies to C.D. Wright

Every year the poem I most want to write, the poem that might in effect
allow me to stop writing, stands at the edge of a field shrouded in mist—
human apparition or tree misshapen by harsh elements. If I invite it to
sit beside me on the porch, it takes a tentative step forward, pulling fog's
hem with it, then retreats. The field between us is grown up in thigh-high
grasses, wildflowers, thistles, pink beach roses with yellow centers. Closer,
the mown lawn is flecked with white clover florets and green blades wet
with dew. A foghorn blasts at regular intervals; clanking buoy keeps time.
Lupines have given way to black-eyed Susans in the rock-edged garden.
Smell of strong black coffee mixes with pine scent and salt sea air, for it
is always August, Maine, a simple boxy pine cottage with clean lines and
wraparound porch, overlooking tidal marsh, sandbar, bay. No coaxing will
entice the poem to inhabit its form, step across the distance, occupy the seat
beside me. And if I should get up to approach this poem, hand extended,
it backs away, shape-shifts, vanishes into the haze.

★

7:VIII:06

Car with Maine plates driving coastal Route 1, sporting bumper sticker:
>"Go Renovate Boston.
>We Like Maine Just The Way It Is."

"Bold Coast" Partita: Sarabande

[Fast and Erotic or Slow Triple Time]

Tire collars around wharf posts, tall sea-damp wooden poles;
    weed-draped netting.

Frayed rope hank, wrist-thick yellow nylon braids, sun-bleached
    wood plinth.

Axe head nicked, auger dulled, jerry can dented, chain link cracked.

Beached dragger, half-submerged, listing with each lapping wave;
    winch, spooled cable, boom all rust-crusted.

Dulse, bladder wrack, pompom, purple laver; barnacle, whelk,
    limpet, periwinkle.

Bivalves in mesh bags, mussels steamed in white wine; glazed
    stoneware bowls.

Quoddy Journal III (2007)

20:VII:07
Six Acts

Distant headland
haze–shrouded
in first light.

Mist peels away
slowly in bands
to reveal the crown
bristling with firs.

Fog thins
while sun climbs,
hand over hand, up
a ladder of branches.

Later,
the jagged shoreline.

Later still,
the hammered silver bay.

To close the show:
splashes of molten gold.

★

21:VII:07

Sweet fragrance of pink and white beach roses
mingled with essence of pine sap—
my preference in cologne.

★

22:VII:07

Rental

Hand-painted Stars & Stripes decorate tissue boxes in every room. White porcelain beer mugs, inscribed "NATIONAL GUARD," stand on a shelf above the kitchen range, three to each side, flanking a beer stein with America's eagle in bas-relief, wings spread wide against a background of flags. "REENLIST" in red letters on a blue banner wraps around its base: "REENLIST," "REENLIST," "REENLIST." Another banner circles the lip. "WARRIORS, " it says, "FIT TO FIGHT," "BE ALL YOU CAN BE." Whose house this is? Why, it's The Colonel's House.

★

23:VII:07

Today my preoccupation
is this cracked, seamed,
frost-heaved, tarmac road
along whose crumbling
shoulders, edged with gravel,
yellow clover
already gone to seed,
squadrons of bees patrol
the hydra-headed chamomile
just coming into flower.

★

24:VII:07

Morning After

Although dark clouds
gather behind me,
I choose to ignore them.

Instead, I pin my hopes
on the risen sun
that right now sits skewered
on the tip of a spruce.

Bushes grown up
since this cabin was built
conspire in whispers.

A breeze animates their leaves,
revealing silvered undersides
while two birches
scratch each other's back.

Beyond the forested ridge,
the chain saw that woke me
has given way to a backhoe
dropping boulders into truck beds.

Man-boy, now sound asleep
under quilts in the loft, I know
that you don't really "hate" me,
or wish to "murder" your mother.

★

25:VII:07

Constitutional

Close book, lace up shoes,
step outdoors, following
the rain-rutted gravel lane
downhill to its terminus
at the asphalt road
along whose crown
a jagged seam runs
trailing off to
crumbled shoulders.

Cautiously descend
the steep bank

tracing a path
through tall grasses
sporting seedy heads,
where someone
previously high-stepped.

This being low tide,
pause at the berm
bordering mudflats
and weed–skirted rocks—
rank salt air:
breathe deeply.

Notice that even pebbles
cast long shadows
in slant morning light.
Observe the bent figures
in waders, raking
the muck for clams
under the supervision
of blue herons.

Start back,
returning the same way,
but as a different person
from the one who came.

★

27:VII:07

A discarded chips bag
lying on the road shoulder,
mustard-color—LAYS
in white script
across a bright red banner—

cannot compete with
hawkweed's yellow petals,
bird's-foot trefoil,
evening primrose;
or—sunniest yellow of all—
buttercups abundant.

★

28:VII:07

Starting from bottom of the drive, travel the winding ribbon of asphalt
hemmed in by scrub brush and stunted conifers that is Boot Cove Road,
enjoying its gentle, roller-coasting dips and rises. Turn at the turnout where
wooden sign fixed to wooden post announces Boot Head Preserve. Follow
the path wending through moss carpets, quaking bog, stands of dwarf fir
and lichen-mottled spruces to where it emerges in Hopperesque light at
eponymous Boot Cove. Note the lone clapboard house perched above
tide-line in the crotch where sheer bluff meets curvant beach; note also
the ancient weir, half submerged; the moored jon boat whose stern the
waves slap. Pick your way along the rocky shore strewn with hanks of
frayed rope thick as your wrist, wood and Styrofoam lobster buoys torn
loose from pots ("Dad, how do they make Styrofoam?"), sun-and-salt
bleached planking, and storm-tossed tree limbs wedged between boulders.
Follow the shoreline, huffing upland to the bluff trail that hugs the high
head all the way to Brooks Cove. Pause. Take in the ocean's expanse, the
sea's languorous swells. Appreciate the solemnity of dead firs stripped bare

of leaves and bark—silvery sentinels, overlooking craggy notches, where
thunderous waves crash below.

★

29:VII:07

Postcard (for Tony Towle in Key West)

Here too, *as if to prove a point*, the sun sets unambiguously
but more like a bloodied yolk than an *overcooked beet*
on a semblance of melted Crayola rather than *poached* exteriors.
Yes, the ocean *gurgitates*,
                          but here it is
hammered pewter instead of *liquefied turquoise*;
and, in place of *ribbons of asphalt and sand*, what's revealed
are graveled ruts and sea-smoothed rocks the size of ostrich eggs.
                       Here we also sing a tune
but not one suited to lolling in *salt sea's bathwater*.
Rather, it is a song of the Maritime north
                         all gasping breaths,
after a quick, scrotum-clenching plunge.

★

30:VII:07

Waves crawl up the steep berm
flipping round flat stones
heads over tails,
then retreat, claws extended,
kneading sand.

Children
run down to water's edge,
giggling,
then turn tail,
screaming with delight
at cold foam's caress.

You, meanwhile, snooze
and read, read
and snooze, umbrella
shading your head
from high noon sun,
sizzling sand's heat
penetrating the blanket
you lie upon.

The frigid sea beckons,
but you decline the invitation,
knowing better—a fist to the chest
that would take your breath away.

To leave or to stay?
That is the question.
Flip a coin; heads or tails.
You call it, I say.
Your nearness
is all I require.

To stay or to leave?
You call it.
Your nearness
is all I require.

★

31:VII:07

Q: What do Revlon nail polish and Buick automobiles have in common?
A: Pearl essence, derived from Lubec herring scales, supplies the shine.
    —#16, from "Things About Lubec You Didn't Know Till Now!"

Where visitors from away (us among them) now wander the sleepy main street, herring, purse-seined in Nova Scotia, were once off-loaded by the hogshead via wooden sluice into these rickety, plank and beam structures perched on pilings. First brined in salt-crusted tubs that needed regular "spudging," the fish were then "sticked" through gill and mouth in strings of twenty and left to drain on racks. Carted to the smokehouse, the strings were then lofted to the rafters and slowly cured over charcoal fires, dusted with sawdust set to smolder with a splash of kerosene. Taken down after the flesh had turned golden, finally, the heads and tails were removed with sharp scissors by women, wearing leather aprons, who "skunned" and packed them in wooden boxes lined with wax paper. Men down the line men nailed on lids and stamped the boxes for shipment to New York, Boston, San Francisco, San Juan, Puerto Rico: *McCurdy's Smoked Atlantic Herring, Lubec, Maine.*

       ★

1:VIII:07

Cloud Inventory

Rude-boy clouds
blown in by the West Wind,
sporting Mohawk hairdos.

Rubenesque billows at sunset—
full figures
softened by the roseate glow.

114

Wads of cotton batting,
wind-pasted to the ridges
of Grand Manan's distant bluffs.

Wispy strands, high above the horizon,
combed back for that period look—
that Pat Boone flip.

★

2:VIII:07

Apologies to Count Théophile Beguin-Billecocq, author of *The
Grand Journal*.

Oh let's go "vagabonding in the environs" like French boys did in
summer at country estates, long ago, "swimming in the ocean, fishing,
going out for lunch and staying out through dinner."
    Whaddaya talking about?
Let's always carrying little notebooks and pencils like they once did
with which to sketch "pastoral landscapes and marines."
    Are you daft?
Let's draw on "every scrap of paper, no matter how small. . . . Every
sheet of paper that [comes] into [our] hands. . . . [preferring] old
papers from the previous century made from real rags."
    Get your head out of the clouds.
And our sketches, oh, our sketches, "whether in crayon, or pencil,
[will be] excellent, even if they were rapidly executed" because only
we know "how to capture the essential characteristics of a scene."
    You're a case for the loony bin.

★

3:VIII:07

Days of cloudless skies and cut glass air
now are memories far off,
obscured by draperies of mist alternating with fog—
fog "thick as oatmeal with a splash of milk stirred in."

Fisherman ahead of me at the gas pump,
taps last drops from the nozzle,
fixes me with his gaze and,
without cracking a smile, offers:
"Best two weeks all summer."

"Bold Coast" Partita: Passacaille

[Continuous Variations on a Ground Bass]

Common Eider meet Common Loon. Common Loon meet Greater Shearwater. Greater Shearwater meet Lesser Scaup. Lesser Scaup meet Wilson's Storm-petrel. Wilson's Storm-petrel meet Hooded Merganser. Hooded Merganser meet Atlantic Puffin. Atlantic Puffin meet Roseate Tern. Roseate Tern meet Black Guillemot. Black Guillemot meet White-winged Scoter. White-winged Scoter meet Ring-billed Gull. Ring-billed Gull meet Double-crested Cormorant. Double-crested Cormorant meet Northern Gannet . Northern Gannet meet Red-necked Phalarope. Red-necked Phalarope meet Harlequin Duck. Harlequin Duck meet Herring Gull. Herring Gull meet Bufflehead. Bufflehead meet Goldeneye. Goldeneye meet Fish Crow. Fish Crow meet Bald Eagle. Bald Eagle meet Osprey. Osprey meet Common Mallard. Common Mallard meet Common Eider.

Quoddy Journal IV (2010)

The summer visitors come to town with a clean shirt
and a ten-dollar bill, and never change either all summer.
—Lubec saying

01:VIII:10

Reveille
Sun at two ticks above horizon, air crystalline
with just a hint of heat haze to come;
not a breath of wind to stir the leaves of trees and bushes;
marsh grasses, roadside weeds, garden flowers. . . .
Rill of a redwing blackbird tests the silence;
a baying hound follows suit.
"Fool," its scolding neighbor barks back,
"*that* ain't the moon!"
 A pickup truck passes, wiping the slate clean.
Start again from scratch; sun now at three ticks.
Crow has something to say about it;
another barking dog finishes the thought.
More tires kissing tarmac;
far off, a ten-wheeler testing its brakes.
Now a great blue heron parachutes to marsh pool mudflat,
folds its wings, strikes a serious pose.
Time to get to work.

★

02:VIII:10
Rental

Renovated fisherman's cottage perched on lip of salt marsh
with views of bay, distant headlands, and sea beyond:
This is not the *Studio of Exhaustion from Diligent Service*,
nor is it the *Belvedere of Viewing Achievements*;
rather it is the *Supreme Chamber for Cultivating Harmony*,
the *Tranquility and Longevity Palace*,
and the *Building for Enjoying Lush Scenery*,
all rolled into one.

★

03:VIII:10
Here lowing Herefords answer the channel foghorn;
hummingbirds probe white hydrangeas;
crows hector other crows,
while harrowers harvest salt hay;
hardhats in pickups
haul ass up gravel lanes,
and hearty hikers traverse
cliffside trails at Quoddy Head.

★

04:VIII:10

Low Tide

No skittering shorebirds, but plenty of clammers raking the mudflats—mudflats scored with shimmering rivulets that run, quicksilver, all the way to the breeze-tickled bay. Overhead, gulls mewling.

From this vantage on fine sand above the high berm, which ends in beach grass and fragrant roses bearing orange hips, the line of sea-wrack downslope looks like a deflated fire hose stretched out in the sun to dry.

And a white-haired couple, dressed identically—Hawaiian shirts and baggy pants—pick their way along the rocky shingle littered with cracked bivalves, spiny urchins, crab shells, claw fragments, sea glass and broken crockery.

The one with walking stick bends, picks up a stone. "Look!" I can just make him out to say, "Look. A dinosaur!" His companion, humoring him, replies, "Yes, yes it is. I can tell by the shape."

★

05:VIII:10
Paradise

Rusted tractor, lobster boat up on blocks,
tall weeds grown up around them,
parked on either side of the garage
at the corner of this gravel lane leading to the marsh.
The lobster boat badly in need of paint,
paint on garage walls weathered, too—
wood grain and knots showing through—

but windows still intact.
Stenciled sign on the door reads:

> *Car Wash*
> ~~*50¢*~~

"twenty-five cents" scrawled below.
This, the street sign says, this is "Paradise Lane."

★

06:VIII:10
On these two-lane blacktop roads absent shoulders,
that rise, dip, and rise again in succession,
straight as the arrow flies through pine and blueberry barrens,
teenagers have left their signatures
in burnt rubber S-shape curves and figure eights—
back country graffiti!

★

07:VIII:10
Sign in window of the Mobil gas and convenience store
announces in bold letters:

> *FREE RIDE*
> *IN SHERRIF'S CAR*

adding, in small print at the bottom:

> *If you are caught*
> *Shoplifting*
> *In this store*

★

08:VIII:10
Inventory

Yellow, white, and purple clover in fields and along road shoulders?

> *Check.*

Joe Pye weed?

> *Check.*

Chamomile?

> *Check.*

Milkweed, Cow vetch, Queen Ann's lace?

> *Check, check, check.*

Pink and white beach roses?

> *Check.*

Indian paintbrush?

> *Check.*

Tansy? Yarrow? Goldenrod? Ox-eye daisy?

> *All check.*

Jewelweed?

> *Check.*

Purple loosestrife?

> *Stop right there, Kemo Sabe!*
> *That's not loosestrife, that's fireweed.*

Right. Got it. . . . Fireweed?

> *Fireweed, check.*

Meadow lily?

> *Check.*

Sweet flag?

> *Check.*

Cattail?

> *Check*

Pitcher Plant?

> *Check.*

Cardinal flower? Throughwort?

> *Both check.*

Cowbane? Hawkbit? Sow thistle?

Check-check-check.
Purple kiss–me–not?
> *Whoa, Kemo Sabe! Wait one second. That's no wildflower;*
> *that's impatiens; busted out of the garden; gone native.*

Impatience?
> *Impatiens! Got it?*

Got it.
That it?
> *That's it!*

★

09:VIII:10
Lunch Break

Kappy's Seafood and Take-out:
"Stop in. Otherwise we'll both go hungry."

★

10:VIII:10
IGA

Two men in pickups,
parked side by side in the IGA lot,
jawing out their driver's-side windows.

One smiling, asks the other
(in a heavy Downeast accent)
"Been in the ditch again lately?"

★

11:VIII:10
Real Estate

Substantial wood-frame house going up at the intersection of First Light and Carrying Cove lanes: two stories high, with windows galore, gables, widow's peak, wraparound porch, two-car garage, brick-paved driveway. . . .

Next lot over, a fisherman's shack, long abandoned: roof falling in; ridge saddle-slumped where the chimney threatens to collapse; weathered clapboards sun-bleached to silver-gray; shutters hanging askew, but a sightline straight through the front windows' absent glazing past the missing back wall to the cove beyond. Parked in the weed-choked gravel driveway, a rusted milk truck, minus doors, windows. Sign planted out front: "For Sale."

★

"Bold Coast" Partita: Bourée

[Quick Duple Time]

"Suits, Clam Boots
Wackies, Khakis
Squid Snaggers
Deadheads & Dreads"—all,

FRANK'S DOCKSIDE RESTAURANT signboard promises—
"All Welcome!"

(No slights intended to mowers, chippers, post-holers, or bush-
hoggers.)

★

Encore

~~"[I]n a mixed vote here on your . . . latest , the 'no's' have it." We found it to be "a little too remote." It "doesn't seem right to us"; "far too special—or perhaps I should say personal"; "too difficult for our readers"; and "a bit too long." It just "doesn't seem quite precise enough"; "we can't help feeling it is more suitable for a literary magazine." But "it may be," very possibly, "our denseness, rather than a real ambiguity in the poem, that led to a negative vote."~~

With regards. Always eager to read more.

★

125

Adieu

Goodbye gray smudge of headland masking the horizon.

So long thin chalk line of fog drawn along its margin.

Auf wiedersehen slate-blue sea marked with imperfect erasures.

Sayonara moss-thatch skullcaps atop granite outcroppings.

Au revoir dripping firs whose needles tickle moisture from
    windblown mist and sea spray.

Ta-Ta boggy riprap trails meandering along cliff edges, surf
    pounding below.

Do widzenia white-knuckle tree roots gripping rock fissures against
    onslaughts of wind, rain, and gale-tossed waves.

Shalom stand of sun-bleached, wind-burnished, silver-white tree
    trunks, impersonating wrathful Tibetan deities.

Ciao chorus lines of roadside grasses whose shaggy hangdog heads on
    long slender necks nod and sway in unison.

Bis spatter silver and white birches trading gossip in stage whispers
    about the prickly pines.

Fins aviat purple-verging-on-pink fireweed standing in pools of
    brackish water.

À bientôt discarded beer cans flattened on road shoulders where truck
    tires have left their impression.

Adios mowers, chippers, bush-hoggers, weed whackers . . . advertising
 services on sandwich boards lining the highway.

Hasta luego tree fellers, clam diggers, purse seiners, oyster shuckers . . .

Salaam scrub trees and bushes whose leaves turn giddy with every breeze.

Salut wind whistling through wires strung between utility poles.

Sale kale scudding billows above white-capped sea swells.

Cheerio channel ferries straining to make headway against Fundy tides.

Arrivederci white clapboard house at shoreline dazzling in early
 morning light.

So long intermittent foghorn; clanking channel buoy.

So long, farewell, *auf wiedersehen*, goodbye.

Adieu. Adieu, to "yieu and yieu and yieu."

Notes:

p.52. "I want you to love me . . ." Lyrics from "Like My Dog" by Billy Currington

p.97. "I just had to jot down these fleeting things . . .": from Isabelle Compin, *H. E. Cross* (Paris, 1964), 6

p.103. C.D. Wright, *Cooling Time: An American Poetry Vigil*

p.112. "Postcard": phrases in italics are from Tony Towle's poem *Song of the South*, part 11 of his 19-part poetic sequence "Illuminations (Diverse Miniatures)."

p.115. The Grand Journal: Comte Théophile Beguin-Billecocq's (1825–1906) son was Monet's dearest friend during his childhood in Le Havre. The quotations describe the boys' summer activities and in particular, Monet's proclivity for sketching on whatever was at hand at all times—from the exhibition catalog *The Unknown Monet: Pastels and Drawings*, by James A. Ganz and Richard Kendall.

p.116. "thick as oatmeal with a splash of milk stirred in."—James Schuyler, *Journals*.

p.118. From *Two Hundred Years of Lubec History, 1776-2006*

p.119. The *Belvedere of Viewing Achievements*, etc.: structures in the Tranquility and Longevity Palace Garden, a private retreat within China's Forbidden City, built by the Qianlong Emperor (r.1736-1796), a connoisseur, scholar and devout Buddhist. He created the luxurious garden compound to serve throughout his retirement as a secluded place of contemplation, repose and entertainment.
    —*from the exhibition catalog, Peabody Essex Museum.*

p.122. **Kemo Sabe**: probably meaning "trusty scout," was how Tonto, Indian sidekick of the Lone Ranger in the radio and TV series, always addressed his masked friend.

p.125. **"[I]n a mixed vote . . .":** *from Elizabeth Bishop and The New Yorker: The Complete Correspondence.*

Acknowledgments

Grateful acknowledgment is made to the editors of the following magazines and anthologies in which versions of these poems previously appeared:

Breakwater Review, Blast Furnace, Boston Mycological Club Bulletin, Consequence, Endicott Review, For the Time Being: The Bootstrap Anthology of Poetic Journals, Hanging Loose, Ibbetson Street, Literature Today, Muddy River Review, Never on Time, New American Writing, New Madrid, No Infinite, On The River: The Cambridge Community Poem (anthology), Off the Coast, Ping Pong, Poetry South, Shampoo, Sixth Finch, Solstice Literary Magazine, SpoKe, StepAway, Temporary Press Annual, and *the Wilderness House Literary Review.*

"Apologies to Rilke" was selected for display at Boston City Hall, April–July 2015 as part of the Mayor's Poetry Program.

"Faith, Hope, Charity" was a featured posting on the Mass Poetry website, Masspoetry.org, May 2015.

Natural Histories appeared as a chapbook published by Cervená Barva Press.

Go to the Pine: Quoddy Journals 2005-2010, appeared as a chapbook published by Bootstrap Press.